T0194952

Hindering Husbands and Helpless Wives

YOUR GUIDE TO A SUCCESSFUL MARRIAGE

Carla F. Robertson-Seaborne

WESTBOW
PRESS®
A DIVISION OF THOMAS NELSON
& ZONDERVAN

WestBow Press books may be ordered through booksellers or by contacting:

WestBow Press
A Division of Thomas Nelson & Zondervan
1663 Liberty Drive
Bloomington, IN 47403
www.westbowpress.com
844-714-3454

Scripture taken from the King James Version of the Bible.

ISBN: 978-1-6642-4022-3 (sc)
ISBN: 978-1-6642-4023-0 (hc)
ISBN: 978-1-6642-4021-6 (e)

Library of Congress Control Number: 2021914089

Print information available on the last page.

WestBow Press rev. date: 8/5/2021

DEDICATION

I dedicate this book to my daddy, Thelma Leon Liverman, Sr., and Evangelist Tony Wilson, my husband of fifteen years. I can testify that these two men have fulfilled the commandment of the Lord. They loved their wives, and they were committed to the task and purpose of Almighty God.

ACKNOWLEDGEMENTS

I thank **Jesus Christ** for allowing me to write this book.

I acknowledge the leaders of **Christ for the World International**, The Fort, in Fort Smith, Arkansas. We traveled to Israel, Mexico, and to churches in many states in the United States.

I thank **Apostle Bobby Hogan and Prophetess Teresa Hogan**, for their labor, prayers, and prophecies.

April Hogan, the word of the Lord that you spoke over my life came to pass. Thanks for your obedient spirit.

Special acknowledgement to **Pastor Jerome Stokes and his wife, Marsha Stokes**. Pastor Stokes, thanks for anointing and praying for me in 2005 on my first mission trip to Africa.

I acknowledge **Elizabeth Hickey** for her financial support.

Trevon Robert Liverman, **Trevous Reggie Liverman**, and **Cortland Matthews**, you have been trained and loved by your grandmother. You will never be forgotten. Your generation needs this book as a guide in marriage and life.

Alfred P. Gladden, author of *Taste Buds Tidbits: What You Eat or What's Eating You? One Man's Revelation*. He worked night and day to instruct, promote, and be my trusted advisor.

We thank one of our own Christian artists, **Willie Moore, Jr.**, for always putting God first, then his wife and children. He is a true family man.

Thank you,

Ebony Kenney, for the website at www.hinderednomore.com;

Calvin Hayes, the photographer, for the picture on About the Author;

Kamau Sennaar, Publication Design Specialist, who designed the cover and did the layout for the book;

Noami Hanna, the artist, for that great illustration of marriage in the book and on the website;

Dorothy Gwynn and **Deborah Mickle**, typists;

Megan Petty for her editing and typing;

Alice Heiserman for her editing; writebooksright.com

Marcellus "The Bassman" Shepard for being the vocal introduction to my website and the voice of my audiobook; themanwiththevo@gmail.com

Hugs to **Fantasia Barrino** for your acknowledgement of the necessity for the wife to be submissive to their husband in spite of backlash.

Kendall Taylor, thanks for the example you provide as leader of your household.

APPRECIATION TO THE AUTHOR

"My daughter, who helps with whatever is needed."
Arnetta Liverman

*"Thank you for the love and togetherness and
for the celebration of family."*
Deniece Davis

"Thank you for being a good mom."
Robert Liverman

*"Thank you, Carla, for making this book a reality. Your faith
and outlook on the natural and spiritual realms speaks volumes of
your commitment to serve God. It is a wonderful testimony of how
couples should be guided. Simply encouraging! Many kisses."*
Dorothy Gwynn

SHALOM

Yahweh (name revealed to Moses, the divine name)

Hebrew Adonay "My Lord" translated as Kyrios

Hebrew

JHVH

Medieval	Latin English
lehouah	Yahweh
lehoug	Tetragrammatom (YHWH) (fl 1100BCE-200 CE) modern and Hebrew scripts
JeHoWaH	In Hebrew Bible too sacred to utter

PRAYER BY CARLA F. ROBERTSON-SEABORNE
FOR READERS

Father in the name of Jesus, we acknowledge you as we embrace the beauty of your spirit. Let your voice echo in our hearts as we give ear to this marriage guide and obey. Let us not ignore, turn away, or disregard the truth. As we enter into covenant committed to each other and your word, we can give thanks for your grace and love toward us, as we communicate with you and each other.

Let us digest the words of this book to improve, grow, and prepare for a record-breaking union ordained by you. Putting in mind that we need your help and faith to walk and live according to the path set before us this day. Not backing up or backing down whether this is your first marriage or a failed marriage. I trust your guidance knowing with you we can accomplish all that is planned for this journey called Life. The ultimate way to receive all the blessings of marriage is by following the Bible.

A picture of a couple walking towards a bright future.

CONTENTS

FOREWORD

This book is for men and women of all nations. Receive your new heart and renew your mind by reading the word of God. God will enlighten your understanding and you will know what God says about marriage.

Five things this book will teach you:

1. You can be transformed by the renewing of your mind.
2. You can love again in a pure and holy way.
3. You can make better decisions that create good results.
4. You can change the course of your life by submitting to the word of God and repenting.
5. You can forgive yourself and those who you have hurt and pray for them.

This book is written to enlighten you—not to condemn you. It will brighten your darkness, and warn you that God does not smile at you when you do not treat your spouse right.

There is so much hope for marriages today. Fear will not preside over, govern, prevail, or control any part of our lives. You will prosper living according to the will of God. We will embrace any obstacle that would come to subdue, overwhelm, or demolish us. So, we rejoice in the hope that makes every marriage successful, trusting God to complete what He began in us.

Use what is in this guide on your journey called marriage. It is meant to encourage you before marriage, and is also for those who have entered into marriage. This book will help you to solve problems and educate and equip you to improve your marriage. The book will open your eyes and soften your heart to appreciate the gift of marriage.

FOUNDATION OF THIS BOOK

The foundation for this book is found in Ephesians, King James Version.

EPHESIANS 5:21-33

- 5:21 "Submitting yourselves one to another in the fear of God"
- 5:22 "Wives, submit yourselves unto your own husbands, as unto the Lord"
- 5:23 "For the husband is the head of the wife, even as Christ is the head of the church: and he is the savior of the body"
- 5:24 "Therefore as the church is subject unto Christ, so let the wives be to their own husbands in everything"
- 5:25 "Husbands, love your wives, even as Christ also loved the church, and gave himself for it"
- 5:26 "That he might sanctify and cleanse it with the washing of water by the word"
- 5:27 "That he might present it to himself a glorious church, not having spot, or wrinkle, or any such thing; but that it should be holy and without blemish"
- 5:28 "So ought men to love their wives as their own bodies. He that loveth his wife loveth himself"
- 5:29 "For no man ever yet hated his own flesh; but nourisheth and cherisheth it, even as the Lord the church"
- 5:30 "For we are members of his body, of his flesh, and of his bones"

- 5:31 "For this cause shall a man leave his father and mother, and shall be joined unto his wife, and they two shall be one flesh"
- 5:32 "This is a great mystery: but I speak concerning Christ and the church"
- 5:33 "Nevertheless let every one of you in particular so love his wife even as himself; and the wife see that she reverence her husband"

It is important to learn a person's likes and dislikes before you marry. This is why it is important to be prepared for marriage. In my view, marriage is a God-given assignment. God presented Eve to Adam for a helpmate.

> *"What therefore God hath joined together, let not man put asunder."*
>
> (Mark 10:9, KJV)

God knows what is good and what is not good. God knew it was not good that Adam was alone. God created Adam from dust and breathed into his nostrils the breath of life. Man became a living being and God placed him in the Garden of Eden. God's plan for marriage was to make a suitable mate for us.

> *"And the rib, which the Lord God had taken from man, made he a woman, and brought her unto the man."*
>
> (Genesis 2:22, KJV)

> *"And Adam said This is now bone of my bones, and flesh of my flesh: she shall be called Woman, because she was taken out of Man."*
>
> (Genesis 2:23, KJV)

Adam received his woman down to the bone. He married her for the soul and not just her body. That's what you call faithful.

> "Therefore shall a man leave his father and his mother, and shall be one flesh."
>
> (Genesis 2:24, KJV)

> "And they were both naked, the man and his wife, and were not ashamed."
>
> (Genesis 2:25, KJV)

PURPOSE OF THIS BOOK

Hindering Husbands and Helpless Wives is a guide for a successful marriage written for people having difficulties in their marriages and for those preparing to get married. Many of today's marriages are failing and people are suffering a great deal because God is not in their midst. We need the word of God to direct us and give us answers for life's most pressing questions: these answers are in the word of God. *Suffering* occurs when we undergo distress, pain, or hardship. We kick God out, but the Bible says, "The blessing of the Lord, it maketh rich, and he added no sorrow with it" (Proverbs 10:22, KJV).

Too often, we follow the patterns of modern society without really looking to God as our source and answer to life's problems and issues. We need God's word, in the form of the Bible, to guide us in our decision-making. Hopefully, this book will inspire and motivate you. This book is for the peacefully married, the unmarried, and for those who are in marriages without peace.

I would encourage single men and women to read this book to find out what they can do to select the right man or woman so they truly will be prepared to have a successful marriage. Those of you who are married, take a critical look at yourselves and make realistic changes to improve your lives. Remember not to be selfish and to care only about your own desires.

I hope you are not a "hindering husband." Yes, a woman can hinder a man as well, but this book focuses on husbands and helpless wives.

God made the husband the head and not the tail, above and not beneath, a leader in the earth. He didn't make him to run after every skirt, to be quick to take off his pants, to jump into every bed, and yet still be unfulfilled in his heart. Just like a storm can hinder traffic, your vision can be blocked, making it hard to see the traffic signs and directions, which can be fatal. Seek God for direction.

Vision is very important. You should see and know where you are going. A hindering husband can kill your dream. Don't let this happen! The duty of the wife is to pray for the husband so that the family can be guided by the Holy Spirit, according to the will of the Father. Submit one to another in the fear of God. If the vision is not clear, you will need to seek God for direction.

Jesus Christ should be first. The instructions go first to the man, the head of the household. That does not mean the Lord does not speak to wives. God spoke through a Donkey to Ba-laam (Numbers 22:28, KJV) and commanded the raven birds to feed Elijah the Tishbite, at the brook

Cherith, east of Jordan, bringing him bread and flesh in the morning and bread and flesh in the evening (1 Kings 17: 1-7, KJV). In this way, the Lord cares for the ones who will seek Him.

This book will bring ruin to the Kingdom of Darkness, and its destruction or disintegration.

"He that committeth sin is of the devil; for the devil sinneth from the beginning. For this purpose, the Son of God was manifested, that he might destroy the works of the devil" (1 John 3:8, KJV).

This book is for all men and women. You are about to get a heart transplant and find some enlightenment.

YOU CAN:

1. Be transformed by the renewing of your mind
2. Make better decisions that create good results

3. Change the course of your life by submitting to Jesus Christ our Savior
4. Be forgiven

Read the Bible daily. It is like taking a bath. Miss a day, a week, or month and your mind, body, soul, and spirit become filthy.

It was in God's plan before the foundation of the world for me to record this book, *Hindering Husbands and Helpless Wives*, on earth.

> *"Oh magnify the Lord with me, and let us exalt his name together"*
>
> (Psalms 34:3, KJV).

The word says in John 12:32, KJV, "And I, if I be lifted up from the earth, will draw all men unto me." John 6:44, KJV, says, "No man can come to me, except the Father which hath sent me draw him: and I will raise him up at the last day." "Draw Father Draw," Zechariah 4:6, KJV, states. "Not by might, nor by power, but by my spirit, saith the Lord of hosts." Be glorified, Lord Jesus! "But, if our gospel be hid it is hid to them that are lost" (2 Corinthians 4:3, KJV). "In whom the God of this world hath blinded the minds of them which believe not, lest the light of the glorious gospel of Christ, who is the image of God, should shine unto them" (2 Corinthians 4:4, KJV). The questions are what image and likeness are shining in your life?

"For God, who commanded the light to shine out of darkness, hath shined in our hearts, to give the light of the knowledge of the glory of God in the face of Jesus Christ. But we have this treasure in earthen vessels, that the excellency of the power may be of God, and not of us" (2 Corinthians 4:6-7, KJV), proclaims.

It is all about Jesus Christ. In Jesus, we win. Some are going to be found naked, not clothed with the truth, because they would rather believe the liar himself, Satan. You are a servant to whom you yield your members to obey. Present yourself to your Creator. He will fix the brokenness and complete the good work He started in you.

Some people may not know what it means to hinder someone. ***Hindering*** means many negative things, such as delaying or obscuring others. You can hinder a person by reacting slowly to their questions or requests, or by clogging up their ability to do their job.

Maybe we tell them we will be home at 5 o'clock in the evening but show up at midnight, not allowing our spouse to go to a meeting because nobody else could watch the children. We might handicap our spouse by constantly accusing her of looking at other men.

We can place obstacles in the way of our spouse by not participating in the disciplining of children, or in a fit of anger tossing down and breaking a plate she likes.

Being a hindering husband takes many forms, but none of them is good.

MY STORY

I can testify to the mighty works of God in my life. In March 1980, I gave my life to the Lord Jesus Christ.

I worked with my then-boyfriend, owner of a nightclub and restaurant. One of my jobs was to cook spaghetti and serve it on Thursday nights. I did not drink or dance. It just so happened that my friend Randy, who was going out with the assistant manager, had given her life to Jesus Christ. She got saved and stopped coming to the club. She started going to church.

Some of those around me thought this was weird. I didn't think that going to church was weird. My question was, "What's wrong with church?"

The reply was, "Carla, it's not just church. She has the Holy Ghost and speaks in tongues." The speaking in tongues was something new to me. I hadn't been exposed to that before. Randy was my friend, and I wanted to see her. Randy came to the club, one Friday night, that I will never forget! My ears popped open as she preached the gospel to me.

For seven days and seven nights Randy welcomed me into her home, and we studied the word of God and prayed together. My soul had been so empty and was so thirsty. I was twenty-five-years-old then. Randy invited me to her church, the Tabernacle of Prayer for All People. I accepted the invitation; thanks be to God. While the preacher was preaching, he invited seven people who needed to be delivered and receive the gift of the Holy Ghost to the front of the church. In my mind I hoped to be one of those people.

Evangelist Benjamin Brown was the preacher for the hour. As I was standing up, and as I began to sit down, the power of God fell on me. I ran around this big church three times at the speed of light. A baby was in the way. My right arm scooped up the baby as I went speeding by. That was my first experience with the power of God. I heard the Lord speak to me, and He said, "Come model for me and say yes to the miracles." At that time, I was modeling in the fashion world and wanted to go to Hollywood, but God had a better plan for my life. I knew it was God because I was shy and would not otherwise have run around the church the way I did that day.

The trials and tribulations I endured during this time were very painful. A lot of them stemmed from ignorance on my part, but I continued to sit on the mercy seat of the Lord Jesus Christ. I cried, "Help me, Lord!" I sanctified myself, thanking God daily, for He has mercy and He showered me with it. And I was, and am, so grateful.

For, I found God. God is not like men. He will not forsake you when times are bad, and when afflictions are many. Weary seasons can bring frustrations and heartache, but I have learned that the ways of God are not as we suppose, but they caused me to lean on Him and trust Him even more.

That was the beginning of my relationship with the Lord Jesus Christ as Savior, and my experience with the Lord. I was saved under a ministry that preached holiness and hell so much that it took me a long time to know the love of God, to see Him as a father and friend. The fear of God and hell was so real.

The persecution through family, friends, and foes was on every side and was intense, but I knew I wanted to continue to learn and grow in the gift that I was blessed with, the Holy Spirit from God. Many did not know how to love, cover, or fight for me. I thank God that the prayers of the righteous prevailed.

What shall we say to these things, if God be for you, who can be against you! One day I was praying, and God asked, who is against you? I have always prayed for my enemies as if I were praying for my mother knowing that God could save them also, and they could convert to the Kingdom of God.

During my evangelistic season, the Lord opened the door for me to be able to evangelize where I got saved. God allowed me to return to the club many years later with my prayer warriors. We shared the gospel of Jesus Christ with the manager and he allowed me to do a prayer breakfast at his restaurant. Then, I started traveling and evangelizing.

I met the man, Tony Wilson, who became my husband at the Tabernacle of Prayer Church in Baltimore, Maryland. We both knew that we were on fire for God, so Evangelist Benjamin Brown married us and we continued to do the work of the Lord.

Evangelist Tony Wilson was a mighty man of God with the gift of discernment and the love of Jesus Christ. Tony was a God-sent blessing. I can count our disagreements on one hand, and those were because he could see the friends I had who were my enemies. My reply was, "I have to love my enemies and friends. I will love them all the same." He was correct about my friends being my enemies. Before Tony went to be with the Lord, we had evangelized for fifteen years.

During this time, we had a church in our home, the Church of Jesus Christ and the Power of God, and we took in more than seventeen families and helped them get saved. One of the seventeen families was that of Apostle Kerry Jones. We worked along with Apostle Kerry Jones to establish the Jesus Christ Prayer and Deliverance Church in downtown Baltimore. We developed an evangelistic team and preached in many churches in Baltimore and on the East Coast. We experienced the quickening power of the Holy Ghost in a powerful way. This was an awesome experience, and I am so happy to have shared those times with them.

You can grieve so long that it can blind you to the purpose of God in your life. I realized that Tony was an idol in my life, and his death proved that. We all know that God is a jealous God, and no one should take the throne of your heart but God almighty. I lost focus, and my vision was not as clear as it should have been, and I slid back in some areas in my life. I thank God that He got me back on track.

Apostle Kerry Jones taught me so much. One major thing I learned is that to lose is to gain in the kingdom. Losing someone you love may seem a tragedy at first, but in death, there is victory. Thank you, Lord. The scripture says, "Being confident of this very thing, that he which hath begun a good work in you will perform it until the day of Jesus Christ" (Philippians 1:6, KJV).

I have tasted the goodness of God, and this has led me to repentance, and He continues to show me grace and have mercy on me. He is my shield and my great rewarder. The good I have done and the bad, the Lord knows and is my judge. Yes, I am sorry for all my sins—known and unknown by others. Now that I know the love of Jesus Christ, I am a lot better than I ever was.

LEARNING TO TRUST GOD ALL THE WAY

Trusting God all the way, in nothing shall I be ashamed.
Carla Faye, that's my name. I love the Lord Jesus Christ.
He died for me and set me free,
An eternal life is prepared for you and me.
He opened my eyes gracefully, and now I can finally see.
Now, I can call upon his name, stepping over all the shame.
Call me what you will or may,
I am learning to trust God all the way.

Chapter 1

GOD'S TRUE PURPOSE
OF MARRIAGE

God wants to equip us in marriage as he does his saints in the body of Christ. We have to guard, instruct, and protect our inner spirit. We must do this by allowing the Holy Spirit to flow in our lives. We must let the apostolic and the prophetic works of the Holy Spirit guide us in our marriages.

> *"Therefore if any man be in Christ, he is a new creature: old things are passed away; behold, all things are become new"*
> (2 Corinthians 5:17, KJV).

We must be established in faith and love in the gospel of Jesus Christ, thereby walking in the unity of the Holy Spirit, which is our strength. God's plan for our marriages is to establish us in truth. So, allow the Lord to confirm the vision and plan for your lives. In essence, we do not want to be uprooted by life's afflictions and sufferings that we encounter on earth. We want to be sure in our marriages.

If you are going to have a successful marriage, read 1 Corinthians 6:15-20, KJV. The Bible says that without faith, it is impossible to please God. We want to please the Lord. "Your body is the temple of the Holy Ghost who is in you, whom you have from God" (1 Corinthians 6:19, KJV).

> "But without faith it is impossible to please him: for he that cometh to God must believe that he is, and that he is a rewarder of them that diligently seek him"
> (Hebrews 11:6, KJV).

We may have to ask, knock on the door, and seek the heart of God. That is the process, but don't faint, quit, or give up on God. We look to him to help us in overcoming every obstacle that would dare to hinder the marriage in any way.

Marriage is a ministry, and we should not cut corners. We should learn to communicate with God first, and then with each other. This process will help us to keep unity, love, and faith in our household.

Some people don't believe in the order—male and female—that God created them. You can't play house, switch roles, and convince yourself that He is backward. Know it's you! You can repent and get saved as well. God knows exactly what He's doing and going to allow. So, don't be found among the ungrateful. "And even as they did not like to retain God in their knowledge, God gave them over to a reprobate mind, to do those things which are not convenient" (Romans 1:28, KJV). If God rejects you, you are done, dead, and you have a very destructive lifestyle, unacceptable to the Father. You have a choice to receive the blessings of the Lord. However, God has no pleasure in the wicked perishing. He gave His life to give us life in the present world, and for eternity.

But some want God and the devil. They may attend church and

then abuse their wife and kids. The instructions are clear, unchangeable, and required by all. But some of us love this present world too much, and there is no light in the marriage or family. Don't you dare glory in appearance and not in the heart.

God knows it all, every hair on your head, every cell in your body, every artery, vein, joint, and muscle. He is the master builder of the human body, soul, and spirit. Help us dear Lord! We too often want the approval of man and not God.

Some people can be very two-faced. We used to say that, "your word is your bond," but without God in your heart, no one can trust your word or your works. We need to change our unfruitful ways and do our best.

Don't be among the people who exhibit unbelief, a proud look, a lying tongue, and hands that shed innocent blood. Beware of those who sow discord among each other, and all other abominations. Don't you quit! There is hope. Repent and give God a chance to redeem you.

YOU NEED A VISION: A VISION FOR YOUR FAMILY

You know that vision is very important. It is the state of being able to see and know where you are going. A hindering husband can kill his family's dreams. God says the people perish for lack of knowledge. Hence, having vision is important for a marriage and family.

Your prescribed order is to learn to set goals, pray daily, communicate daily, and have weekly home meetings with each family member to find out what each person is dealing with, to resolve issues or concerns, and to accomplish each goal. Do not listen to the bad advice of outsiders or employ witchery when it comes to the goals and values of your family. It is important to stay focused on God's will for you and your family.

The Holy Bible is your medication. The great physician is Jesus Christ, God Almighty, " …with God all things are possible" (Matthew 19:26, KJV). What is impossible to man is possible with God. For example, you may say, Oh, my marriage is a mess, there are too many broken pieces; it's hopeless. Where is your faith? You must speak life to live, love to heal, and not go by what you feel. Seek God's will! Some marriages could have survived if only you knew or had read a guide.

Life is a journey of faith. Read the Bible to find hope. Attend church to keep growing. Seek counsel from your pastor. When storms come, you may suffer a loss of material possessions, but to be alive, there is always hope of rebuilding and having a fresh start. A spouse may go home with the Lord, but your faith says God knows best.

To every thing there is a season, and a time to every purpose under the heaven: (Ecclesiastes, 3:1, KJV)

A time to be born, a time to die; a time to plant, a time to pluck up that which was planted; (Ecclesiastes. 3:2, KJV)

A time to kill, a time to heal; a time to break down, and a time to build up; (Ecclesiastes 3:3, KJV)

A time to weep, a time to laugh; a time to mourn, and a time to dance; (Ecclesiastes 3:4, KJV)

A time to cast away stones, a time to gather stones together; a time to embrace, a time to refrain from embracing; (Ecclesiastes 3:5, KJV)

A time to get, a time to lose; a time to keep, a time to cast away; (Ecclesiastes 3:6, KJV)

A time to rend, a time to sow; a time to keep silent; a time to speak; a time to love, a time to hate; a time of war, and a time of peace. (Ecclesiastes 3:7, KJV)

We should appreciate our life and our ability to use our limbs and be active in the daily duties of life for they are a gift from God.

CHARACTER

Character is very important. Character includes both mental and moral issues. It is important to pay attention to how your prospective spouse treats you and others. Core values are very important. How do your decisions and actions align? You need the following things:

- Hope: an optimism that God is always there
- Justice: for all, not just your share
- Service: helping others, not just seeking to help yourself.

A marriage is stressed when you have to deal with a male with no morals, or one who lacks respect and is rude. Seek God before and during marriage, not only when a marriage fails. Character includes the mental and moral qualities distinctive to an individual, temperament, psyche, as well as the traits, essence, uniqueness, and qualities that a person has.

Marriage ordained by God might not be approved by the family. Friends may be jealous as well. However, God brings blessings to us as divine connections.

In the Old Testament, (Genesis 25:19-34, KJV) Isaac prayed for his wife Rebecca to conceive. She bore twins. The twins were Esau and Jacob, and Prophecy held that the older would serve the younger but through deception of Rebecca, Jacob stole Esau's birthright. So, Esau wanted to kill Jacob who stole his blessing. Jacob, out of the fear of his life, was running away. He ran into Laban and that is where he fell in love at first sight with Rachel, Laban's youngest daughter. Laban deceived Jacob and gave him Leah as his wife, which made Jacob very unhappy because Leah was tender-eyed and Rachel was who he loved and was beautiful and well favored.

Leah became one of the two wives of the patriarch Jacob. She spent most of her time weeping and praying to God to change her husband.

God saw that Leah was not loved, because Jacob expected to marry her sister.

When the Lord saw that Leah was hated, He opened her womb: but Rachel was barren (Genesis 29:31, KJV). Leah had six sons and a daughter (Genesis 35:23, KJV). Rachel, the sister who Jacob loved, was barren but finally got pregnant and died giving birth. Rachel's death occurred before Leah died (Genesis 35:16-18, KJV). God is just; He sees and judges according to His mercy. God sees the root of every matter and is righteous.

Families can have perverted mindsets and engage in incest marrying close cousins and other family members, which are forbidden relationships before God.

Just remember the story of evil Nimrod, the mighty hunter, who married his mother Semiramis, also known as Ishtar and Isis in his rebellion against God. (Genesis 10: 8-12, KJV). "And Ham saw the nakedness of his father [Noah], and told his two brethren without" (Genesis 9:22, KJV).

The daughters of Lot had sex with their father while he was drunk. "And they made their father drink wine that night also: and the younger arose, and lay with him; and he perceived not when she laid down, nor when she arose." (Genesis 19:35, KJV) "Thus were both of the daughters of Lot with child by their father." (Genesis 19:36, KJV)

Know in your own life that God can help you if you seek His guidance and act in the way He prescribes. You can turn your hearts back to the Lord and become faithful before you reach an age where you are unable to help others. Every minute and every hour is important. Just repent and seek deliverance.

"Husbands, love your wives, even as Christ also loved the church, and gave himself for it."
(Ephesians 5:25, KJV)

Chapter 2

PREPARATION FOR MARRIAGE

Marriage is not just sex and fun. Marriage is a legal union or formally recognized union of two people. Marriage is ordained by God.

It is important to prepare for marriage prior to getting married. And, once you are married, you may need a tune-up to help you keep your marriage running smoothly. Should you need extra encouragement, there are workshops and special Christian couples' weekends to help you rekindle the love you once felt.

When preparing to get married, the first principle is to assess **WHO** you are getting your instructions from in your marriage preparations. God is who you should be listening to for guidance and direction in your marriage. To do this successfully, you must have a relationship with Him and His son, Jesus Christ, and the Holy Spirit.

Second, you must know **WHAT** to do in your marriage. These principles will only come from the Word of God, which you must read daily to know His will for your life.

Knowing **WHEN** to know what to say and do, and knowing what not to say and do is important. You will only understand this behavior through the guidance of the Holy Spirit. He will direct you and lead you into all truth, and that will show you a path to a better relationship.

When it comes to **WHERE**, it is important in your marriage to attend church services together. "And Jesus knew their thoughts, and said unto them, every kingdom divided against itself is brought to desolation; and every city or house divided against itself shall not stand" (Matthew 12:25, KJV). It is important for a husband and wife to be on the same page as a family. Although you may have a pastor or overseer, they are not always right about issues relating to your family. However, it is always important to seek the Holy Spirit for help and guidance for all issues.

HOW to have a successful marriage. We have to prepare. Again, we are to put God first in our lives, and study and obey the laws and statutes of God. We are to learn to respect each other, be patient, have long suffering, and be gentle, kindhearted, and giving of ourselves. Do not bring past relationships or past hurts into a new relationship.

You cannot marry and be in love with someone else just for convenience or out of spite. One should not enter into the marriage partnership based on wrong motives, such as marrying for money, for security, or simply for beauty. Seek the Lord for your spouse. When two are unequally yoked, and have not asked the Lord for guidance, then you will open the door for a failed marriage. You must be prepared to invest both your energy and time.

People are unequally yoked when they do not agree on their religious beliefs. For example, if a man does not accept Jesus Christ as his Savior and his wife does, there will be problems living their life as a couple according to Biblical teachings. Their core values are not aligned, and they are likely to have many arguments and tension in their household. When two are yoked, God will show the way.

Another step is to consider your parents' marriage. Was it happy? Did it bring joy to the family?

If it helped people recognize their relationship to God, then you can emulate it. If it did not, then you will need pastoral counseling so you don't make the same mistakes, because you were shown the wrong role model.

Marriages built around God are sweet and joyful. Marry fellow believers—don't be unevenly yoked. "Neither shalt thou make marriages with them; thy daughter thou shalt not give unto his son, nor his daughter shalt thou take unto thy son" (Deuteronomy 7:3, KJV). "The wife is bound by the law as long as her husband liveth; but if her husband be dead, she is at liberty to be married to whom she will; only in the Lord" (1 Corinthians 7:39, KJV). "Be ye not unequally yoked with unbelievers: for what fellowship has righteousness with unrighteousness? And what communion has light with darkness. (2 Corinthians 6:14)?

Take a long-term view of marriage. You will be together for many years, and you should focus on the harmony of your beliefs—not such things as beautiful bodies.

Some people marry due to sexual attraction. While this is certainly important in a matrimonial union, it is insufficient to support a marriage in the long run. The lust of the flesh is inadequate to sustain a relationship, especially when there are other problems, and in a marriage there will always be other problems.

Don't marry someone thinking you will be able to change that person. Be aware of the other person's limits and weaknesses. If you can't accept the person for who he or she is now, it is better not to get married.

When we marry, we enter into a covenant relationship with God. A covenant relationship in marriage is an agreement between you, your spouse, and God.

You are obligated by God almighty to bear fruit, love your neighbor as yourself, and help stop suffering and pain. Don't be guilty of deliberately hurting each other. Be sensitive in your mind and spirit toward your spouse. Two is better than one. When you lose a partner, you want the report that you gave the marriage your all.

Don't engage in marriage before you know what God has to say about marriage. The Lord gave us instructions. We must follow Christ Jesus to receive His blessings.

Women will have a problem submitting to a man when they are unequally yoked. Can two walk together, except if they agree (Amos 3:3, KJV)?

Couples must be able to be as one flesh. "Husbands, love your wives, even as Christ also loved the church, and gave himself for it" (Ephesians 5:25, KJV). The Word of God is right. The mind of the Spirit for the family is clear. He gave His life for His bride.

"Likewise, ye husbands, dwell with them according to knowledge, giving honor unto the wife, as unto the weaker vessel, and as being heirs together of the grace of life; that your prayers be not hindered" (1 Peter 3:7, KJV).

"But if any provide not for his own, and especially for those of his own house, he hath denied the faith, and is worse than an infidel" (1 Timothy 5:8, KJV).

"Live joyfully with the wife whom thou lovest all the days of the life of thy vanity, which he hath given thee under the sun, all the days of thy vanity; for it is thy portion in this life and in thy labour which thou takest under the sun" (Ecclesiastes 9:9, KJV).

For the man, a good man's concern is to be good to his wife and to provide whatever is needed. "But he that is married careth for the things that are of the world, how he may please his wife" (1 Corinthians 7:33, KJV).

Make a covenant with your eyes to God to be faithful to your wife only. "But I say unto you, that whosoever looketh on a woman to lust after her hath committed adultery already in his heart" (Matthew 5:28, KJV).

If you are going to have a successful marriage, read 1 Corinthians 6:15-20. The Bible says that without faith it is impossible to please God. We want to please the Lord, "What? know ye not that your body is the temple of the Holy Ghost which is in you, which ye have of God, and ye are not your own? For ye are bought with a price: therefore glorify God in your body, and in your spirit, which is of God's." (1 Corinthians 6:19-20, KJV).

"But without faith it is impossible to please him: for he that cometh to God must believe that he is, and that he is a rewarder of them that diligently seek him" (Hebrews 11:6, KJV).

Chapter 3

THE RESPONSIBILITIES
OF A GODLY WOMAN

Remember, as the sons and daughters of God, our job is to destroy the works of the devil and the kingdom of darkness. We must bring to ruin the work of the enemy. The God of Peace, Jesus Christ, was wounded for our transgressions. He was bruised for our iniquities, and the chastisement of our peace was upon Him so grace would be with us. "For there is one God, and one mediator between God and men, the man Christ Jesus" (1 Timothy 2:5, KJV).

With the death of Christ on the cross, the veil was torn in two. "And, behold, the veil of the temple was rent in twain from top to bottom; and the earth did quake, and the rocks rent;" (Matthew 27:51, KJV). Let us therefore come boldly unto the throne of grace that we may obtain mercy, and find grace to help in the time of need Now we have an unrestricted access to the throne of God. (Hebrews 4:16, KJV). We are his sons and daughters (2 Corinthians 6:18, KVJ) "And will be a father unto you, and ye shall be my sons and daughters, saith the Lord almighty." The heavens declare the glory of God; and the firmament sheweth his handiwork" (Psalms 19: 1, KJV). What a mighty God we serve.

Satan, "the thief," wants to steal and kill, and then destroy, our marriages. If you are out of alignment with God, the order of your house is compromised. That is a door through which the enemy can destroy your family. There is no mercy when you give place to the devil. He will seduce your husband, which brings reproach on the family unit, so that the family may never recover. The devil may provide a fatal blow, to forever knock you off course.

Know your assignment as a wife. If your husband will not surrender to the will of the Father, the wife will suffer because rebellion is as the sin of witchcraft, and stubbornness is an iniquity and idolatry. Because thou hast rejected the word of the Lord, he has also rejected thee from being king (1 Samuel 15:23, KJV). God will not make your husband serve Him. However, a wife through her example may bring about a change. The choice is but the devil, a killer who is not playing with you. So, it is up to you to fight the good fight of faith and lay hold of the eternal life. Jesus gives abundant life.

The Lord is with us and God knows our hearts. "I the Lord searched the heart" (Proverbs 27:19, KJV) Joseph was a goodly, handsome, prosperous man, and the master saw that the Lord was with him and made him overseer in his house and over all in the field. "And his master saw the Lord was with him, and that the Lord made all that he did to prosper in his hand" (Genesis 39:3, KJV). "And it came to pass after these things, that his master's wife cast her eyes upon Joseph; and she said, 'Lie with me. But he refused'" (Genesis 39:7-8, KJV). Joseph asked how he could do such a great wickedness and sin against God? Leaving his garments in her hand, he fled outside (from Genesis 39:12, KJV). Run from sin. Don't let the evil in. "Submit yourselves therefore to God. Resist the devil, and he will flee from you" (James 4:7, KJV).

The woman must respect her husband. However, the most important duty of the wife is to submit to her husband. The ultimate decisionmaker in the household should be the man, and he should know the will of God for his family. If in disagreement, the Bible is always the guide. That is why prayer is vital. "Trust in the Lord with all thine heart; and lean not unto thine own understanding and in all thy ways acknowledge him, and he shall direct thy paths. Be not wise in thine own eyes; fear the Lord, and depart from evil" (Proverbs 3:5-7, KJV). **You are married to Jesus until you get a husband.**

A wife is there to help. What does it mean to be a helpmate? The dictionary defines a helpmate as a helpful companion or partner who goes out of her way to be responsible. For improving your relationship, you carry a title "wife" then you should be supportive and responsible. A husband has a significant and important role in the household. The husband is the planner, the decision-maker, and the protector in a marriage; that is a role that God gave him. He is a leader, Godly, trustworthy, loyal, and committed. He will give up his life for his spouse. "Therefore shall a man leave his father and his mother, and be joined to his wife, and they shall become one flesh" (Genesis 2:24, KJV). If you are all about you, repent now.

PROVERBS PROVIDES THE MODEL FOR THE GODLY WOMAN

By studying the words of Proverbs about women, we can find the outline of what the Godly woman should be. Consider each line and see how you compare to the Godly woman described in Proverbs 31:10-31 (KJV).

PROVERBS

"Who can find a virtuous woman? For her price is far above rubies"
(Proverbs 31:10, KJV).

"The heart of her husband doth safely trust in her, so that he shall have no need of spoil"
(Proverbs 31:11, KJV).

"She will do him good and not evil all the days of her life"
(Proverbs 31:12, KJV).

"She seeketh wool, and flax, and worketh willingly with her hand"
(Proverbs 31:13, KJV).

"She is like the merchants' ships; she bringeth her food from afar"
(Proverbs 31:14, KJV).

"She riseth also while it is yet night, and giveth meat to her household, and a portion to her maidens"
(Proverbs 31:15, KJV).

"She considereth a field, and buyeth it: with the fruit of her hands she planteth a vineyard"
(Proverbs 31:16, KJV).

"She girdeth her loins with strength, and strengtheneth her arms"
(Proverbs 31: 17, KJV).

"She perceiveth that her merchandise is good: her candle goeth not out by night"

(Proverbs 31:18, KJV).

"She layeth her hands to the spindle, and her hands hold the distaff"

(Proverbs 31:19, KJV).

"She stretcheth out her hand to the poor; yea, she reacheth forth her hands to the needy"

(Proverbs 31:20, KJV).

"She is not afraid of the snow for her household: for all her household are clothed with scarlet"

(Proverbs 31:21, KJV).

"She maketh herself coverings of tapestry; her clothing is silk and purple"

(Proverbs 31:22, KJV).

"Her husband is known in the gates, when he sitteth among the elders of the land"

(Proverbs 31:23, KJV).

"She maketh fine linen, and selleth it; and delivereth girdles unto the merchant"

(Proverbs 31:24 KJV).

"Strength and honour are her clothing; and she shall rejoice in time to come"

(Proverbs 31:25, KJV).

"She openeth her mouth with wisdom; and in her tongue is the law of kindness"
(Proverbs 31:26, KJV).

"She looketh well to the ways of her household, and eateth not the bread of idleness"
(Proverbs 31:27, KJV).

"Her children arise up, and call her blessed; her husband also, and he praiseth her"
(Proverbs 31:28, KJV).

"Many daughters have done virtuously, but thou excellest them all"
(Proverbs 31:29, KJV).

"Favour is deceitful, and beauty is vain: but a woman that feareth the LORD, she shall be praised"
(Proverbs 31:30, KJV).

"Give her of the fruit of her hands; and let her own works praise her in the gates"
(Proverbs 31:31, KJV).

ROLE OF THE HUSBAND TO THE GODLY WOMAN

A husband is to be highly respected, and when he speaks, his wife should listen. He protects and shields his wife. If he does this, he will have blessings of a successful, fruitful, and joyful marriage. If a man is able to exhibit this type of image in his marriage, the results will fit what God's established plan for marriage was from the beginning.

NO GOSSIPING

When you want to gossip to others about your spouse, stop yourself. Talking to another man or another woman about your marriage is an open door for Satan to destroy your marriage. Keep your mind and mouth shut and learn to pray to God. He is a counselor, comforter, and friend in times of need. God solves problems. "Cast thy burden upon the Lord, and he shall sustain thee: he shall never suffer the righteous to be moved" (Psalms 55:22, KJV).

WATCH YOUR TONGUE

The Bible says that "but the tongue can no man tame; it is an unruly evil, full of deadly poison (James 3:8, KJV). We say hurtful things to our spouse, and words have power. You can heal or kill with words. Know when to say something and how to say it. We should learn to edify, exalt, and comfort one another. This is pleasing to the Lord, Jesus Christ.

AN EXERCISE

Take an apple and slice it in half. Notice how one-half of the apple goes one way while the other half goes in the opposite direction. Remember what the action of separating something into parts or the process of being separated causes. A whole is now divided. There is a breach in the covenant, a brokenness, disunity, and division. The worst of these is divorce.

GUIDANCE IN YOUR TRANSFORMATION

You can be transformed by the renewing your mind through the word of God.

The Bible will do all that and more. "Now faith is the substance of things hoped for, the evidence of things not seen" (Hebrews 11:1, KJV).

You can make better decisions by putting God first in order to get better results. God is our substance that we all need in order to succeed.

You can change the course of your life by submitting to Jesus Christ, the Savior.

You can be forgiven for all your sins and all that you have done to cause harm to others.

Release yourself from feeling guilty for failure and disobedience to God when you should have listened.

Don't say harmful things.

Give your best even when you know you are not loved.

Guard your heart and mind against betrayal and pray for those who use you spitefully.

Women with discernment know when their helpmate is cheating. It's painful, but it is better to focus on your assignment and allow God to judge adultery. He will, that's His word.

We have perfect peace when we keep our minds on the Lord Jesus Christ. Watch distractions; know the enemy of your soul.

> "For we wrestle not against flesh and blood, but against principalities, against powers, against the rulers of the darkness of this world, against spiritual wickedness in high places. Wherefore take unto youth whole armour of God that ye may be able to withstand in the evil day, and having done all, to stand"
> (Genesis 6:12-13, KJV).

Women, if you are being physically abused, beaten, cursed out all day long, put down, disrespected, fighting with your husband, and frightened, or you are forgotten by your husband, you have a hindering husband.

God created you to receive love from your husband. The abuse must stop, and you must be aware that abuse is not God's way. A real husband will seek the heart of God for the family and love his wife and children. You should be able to train your children in the household that they may view and experience love as in accordance with God.

If your husband is an uncaring individual with no compassion, or is a non-working and irresponsible being, that is unacceptable behavior. These attributes define him as a hindering husband and his behavior must change. A woman with a husband with these characteristics must seek God for the wisdom to address her hindering husband.

"Nevertheless let every one of you in particular so love his wife even as himself; and the wife see that she reverence her husband" (Ephesians 5:33, KJV). No man or woman should be tormented or wounded because of their spouse's lack of love or patience, and greed or a destructive mindset.

What can a Godly woman do about a hindering husband?

The first step is to seek God. It is best to do this with your spouse.

Sometimes both husband and wife need to learn to communicate better. Instead of yelling at him—"You make me so mad. You're a loser."—the wife might instead say, "I feel hurt when you do not talk to me and just go out and get drunk." There are helpful programs for families of alcoholics such as Al-Anon, and many programs run by or in local churches, such as Alcoholics Anonymous (AA). Even though these programs exist, I have friends who were delivered by the touch of God's hands without going to any program just faith and prayer.

This shift from you to I involves a change in attitude that allows the other person to realize he causes a personal reaction in the other person that disrupts the Holy Spirit.

While calling a person a name or cursing them may be temporarily satisfying, it throws a big roadblock in the relationship that does not allow the blessings of God to enter.

Sometimes the husband may feel ashamed of what he has done. If so, remind him that God loves sinners, and if he repents and wants to change, there is a way for him to do so.

A Godly wife can assure her hindering husband that she will stand by him and work with him to help him rekindle the love of our Savior.

Sometimes, a counselor can help the couple understand their problems and come up with some workable solutions. If a husband refuses to attend counseling, the wife can still go and learn some techniques and approaches that would be useful that she might employ.

A SERIOUS CHARACTER DEFECT

You have a serious character defect,
because you can't get the drugs you love.
You're entangled in an adulterous affair.
You're unfaithful and blue,
and you don't know what to do.
You just don't like God's design.
Remember, He created man and woman and said it
was good.
You're dominating and controlling,
Wanting your way, rejecting the Bible every day.
You're rebellious and hard-hearted. All you want to do,
is you.
You don't hear God or those He sent your way.
You're so immature, you'd rather watch TV, play games,
and have fun all day.
You won't work. Lazy, my father would say,
"Use your head for more than a hat rack."
The Lord is not slack.

You're on the throne alone, and God is nowhere to be found.

You have a bad attitude.

You're full of pride, and quick to say, I don't need a guide.

I'll go my way."

You're not a good guy.

You're violent and have an ugly spirit.

You deal treacherously with your wife.

That's what I call a wasted life.

"After two previous failed marriages that both ended in divorce, this study guide has now educated me on the complexity of marriage, the way God intended it to be His standard."
— *Alfred P. Gladden*

Chapter 4

THE HINDERING HUSBAND

Ask yourself, are you a hindering husband or a heaven-sent husband? Hindering means causing difficulties for someone or something that result in a delay or obstruction, or even destruction.

Do you ever interfere with your wife?
Do you abuse her physically?
Do you abuse her mentally?
Do you put restraints on whom she talks with, where she goes, or when she must be home?

Some men have abused, accused, and battered their wives. They have broken their spirits and wounded their hearts, and cursed them since the day they were married. Fear now rules in the hearts of many women from their hindering husbands who have not loved their wives in the way God intended.

WHOSE CHARACTER DO YOU POSSESS?

Evaluate Yourself

Is your character Christ-like or like the devil?
What is your priority as a man with a family?

God's design is that you guide your family, provide for them, and be a leader to them.

HINDERING

H You are hurting your wife
I Image is false, not scriptural
N Not acceptable, naughty, not nice
D Deadly results
E Eternal consequences
R Ruthless, unrepentant
I Ignorance abounds
N Negative energy floods the relationship
G Godless, ungodly man will not lay down his life for his wife

H Helpers of one another
U United as one flesh
S Spouse is special
B Burden, barrier and best friend
A Answer to prayer
N Necessary part of your wife
D Duty to work and support
S Support your wife

"Favor is deceitful and beauty is vain, but a woman that feareth the LORD, she shall be praised."

Proverbs 31:30 (KVJ)

WEAK BACK-JELLY BACK MAN

You should be leading and working,
Not winking, blinking, and the bed stinking!
Are you in the bed with the wrong head
And not led, children not fed, and sorry you wed?
God can fix the mess.
He told Hosea to marry
And I am sure, he was at heaven's door.
God's ways are not our ways.
I'm sure Hosea prayed,
Lord, guide me with this wife
Who has entered into my life.
Husbands, you don't have to be a weak back, jelly back,
no back kind of man.
On Christ the solid rock, you can stand and be that
God man.
So, stand up man,
Be a man of God.
Read the book,
Stick to the plan,
God says, "Stand."
The Bible tells you what to do.
God says you can look, but get hooked.
Remember what the Bible said,

"Whoso findeth a wife findeth a good thing, and obtaineth forever favour of the Lord"

(Proverbs 18:22, KJV).

MEN, TAKE A STAND

Give no place to the Devil, and if you're the man, take
a stand.
The Holy Ghost has a plan.
Your wife should not limp and you are not a pimp.
So, stand in God.
He will not lead you wrong.
God will not lie.
Some say men "don't you cry."
But it's alright, it's part of the fight.
The Lord is always right!
This is about eternal life.

Christ said we must learn to uplift our spouse and encourage them. We are to allow God to rebuild, reinstate, and show us how to be a champion for our spouse.

We must change our way of thinking from the wrong mindset, and most importantly to change from our will to God's will. We must not allow Satan to cripple us with words, or actions, that do not represent the best we can be. Instead of blowing the oxygen out of your spouses' nostrils, stay connected to the source on the earth, which is the Holy Spirit, which is our Comforter, and He will lead and guide us into all the truth.

Of course, a husband is a married man considered in relation to his spouse. It is best if he considers her his helpmate or better half. When a man is not operating in the principle of the Bible, he is stopping or impeding God's purpose in his life. Therefore, it is always important

that the man not be a hindrance to his family. The only way to stop being a hindrance requires the man to fully execute God's Biblical principles. When a man is operating in Godly principles, his family must respect, appreciate, and support what he does for them.

Remember to place God first in your life. He left His word with you to be a guide for you. As the man of the house, you should seek Jesus Christ first. It is important for you to submit to God as Christ loved and submitted to the church.

Will you lay down your life for your wife? Are you destroying your wife? **THIS IS HUGE!** Can your wife trust you to love her? Is your wife being treated as a priceless queen? "Her husband is known, when he sitteth among the elders of the land" (Proverbs 31:23, KJV). Are you known in the Gates to love your wife or are you bitter? Do you listen to your wife? Do you serve your wife or is it all about you? Do you have your wife's respect? Are you praising your wife or other women? You are just offensive!

"Seeing, we are also compassed about with so great cloud of witnesses, let us lay aside every weight and the sin which doth so easily beset us, and let us run with patience the race that is set before us Looking unto Jesus, the author and finisher of our faith, who for the joy that was set before him endured the cross, despising the shame, and is set down at the right hand of the throne of God" (Hebrews 12:1-2, KJV).

A KINGDOM DIVIDED AGAINST ITSELF CANNOT STAND

The Bible says that, "a kingdom divided against itself, that kingdom cannot stand. And if a house be divided against itself, that house cannot stand" (Mark 3:24-25, KJV).

Marriage is difficult when you are not seeking God. There are several things a couple can do to strengthen one another. We are in a spiritual war and marriage is an assignment.

Do not devour and hurt each other. Repent. When we bite each other, curse each other, despise each other, and are jealous of each other, or sow discord among each other, that is what the Lord hates.

Learn to speak life to what is dead in your marriage. We can speak life and resolve problems of sex, finances, lack of love, communication, misunderstanding, or children. Have hope in God. Find faith, life, and love in Jesus Christ. Be thankful, forgiving, long-suffering, kind, and patient. In essence, be the fruit of the Spirit. The word of God says in Galatians 5:22-23, KJV, to control yourselves. Practice forbearance, kindness, goodness, and self-control.

Practice kindness. It is necessary to trust your spouse. "But the fruit of the Spirit is love, joy, peace, long suffering, gentleness, goodness, faith, meekness, temperance: against such there is no law" (Galatians 5:22-23, KJV).

Also show patience because no one knows everything. Learn to work together, be united in your mind. Where there is unity, there is strength. Love is of God. Love quiets. "Charity suffereth long, and is kind; charity envieth not; charity vaunteth not itself, it is not puffed up, Doth not behave itself unseemly, seeketh not her own, is not easily provoked, thinketh no evil. Rejoiceth not in iniquity, but rejoiceth in the truth" (1 Corinthians 13:4-6, KJV).

"Because the carnal mind is enmity against God: for it is not subject to the law of God, neither indeed can be" (Romans 8:7, KJV). We must mortify the deeds of the flesh. The word marriage should be honorable. "Woe unto them that call evil good, and good evil, that put darkness for light, and light for darkness, that put bitter for sweet and sweet for bitter!" (Isaiah 5:20, KJV). "We serve … the creature instead of the Creator … who changed the truth of God into a lie, and worshipped and served the creature more than the Creator, who is blessed forever …" (Romans 1:25, KJV).

Chapter 5

RESPONSIBILITIES OF
A GODLY MAN

We will describe some responsibilities of a Godly man. There are many assignments that a man does in his life as it relates to his family. Here are some descriptions to explain the divine role and responsibilities of a man to his wife and a father to his children. A man is appointed to be a husband to his wife and a father to his children. You are to hush the cries of your wife and wrap your arms around your family to protect, provide, and aid in their survival.

1. A man is head of the household.
2. A man is a leader.
3. A man is a protector.
4. A man is a provider.
5. A man is a sacrificial lamb.
6. A man is a visionary.
7. A man is a creator for his family.

8. A man is a strategic planner.
9. A man is a possessor of the land.

A man's primary responsibility is to love his wife as Christ loved the church. A man can never love his wife unless he is first in love with Christ and himself. Therefore, it is critical that a man is with Christ and follows the divine instructions in the word of God to receive the blessings of the Creator.

As the head of the household, you must always be mindful of your role in the family. The family is looking up to you. They're looking for you to be that rock, just as Christ was the rock for the church. It is important as the man of the house to be obedient and seek guidance from the Lord. Jesus Christ was obligated to do to the will of the Father.

You will be held accountable to God for bad behavior. When you are out cheating, stealing, acting slick and sly, and being all the things that God did not create, or if you do not care to provide, not only does your family fall, but other families fall as a result of your bad example. The family is God's purpose on earth. It is important to live out this purpose in accordance with the laws of God. "For the wages of sin is death; but the gift of God is eternal life through Jesus Christ our Son" (Romans 6:23, KJV).

A HUSBAND'S ROLE—BEGINS IN THE MIND

"Let this mind be in you, which was also in Christ Jesus" (Romans 2:5, KJV).

The transformation begins in the mind. You obtain the proper mindset from reading the Bible, which is God's design. Your destiny is attached to the decisions you make. Sure, we have all made bad decisions, but thanks be to God, we can choose to change the course of our lives by submitting to Jesus Christ our Savior. You, as head of the household, must be adamant like Joshua, not wavering, "but as for me and my house, we will serve the Lord" (Joshua 24:15, KJV).

As discussed earlier, vision is very important. If a family does not have a vision, they will truly perish. Husbands please don't kill the vision; don't kill the dream; don't destroy or disable your bride. Put away your foolish pride. Humble yourself before your God and pray; that's what brightens a day! "We are to write the vision, and make it plain upon tables, that he may run that readeth it" (Habakkuk 2:2, KJV). So, men, the baton is in your hand!

As the man of the house, you alone set the tone of the household. Despite whatever else is happening in the world, you are to put on the whole armor of God, which is the word of God. You are to be the decision-maker for your family. As a family you are to follow the path of God's principles by walking in love and righteousness. Choose life, not death.

Pray until you have a clear view of your direction. Make sure that when you and your wife are in disagreement, you are an unstoppable force. This may seem like an awesome responsibility, but remember, God has already given you dominion to possess everything you need, as long as you continue to operate in His will. Remember, He did not think it was good for man to be alone, so he sent you a wife.

In second Samuel Chapter 11, David didn't leave the palace to go to war with his men; instead, David stayed at home to have an affair with Bathsheba. Every day we choose to walk in the spirit, or in the flesh.

The appetite of the flesh is different from the appetite of the spirit. "Man shall not live by bread alone, but every word that proceedeth out of the mouth of God" (Matthew 4:4, KJV). Flesh cries and refuses to die. Then, we blame God and say, "Lord why?" Repent. Don't you try, He did it for you when they cried "crucify." His flesh died, his love was stronger than death. "If you love me, keep my commandments" (John 14:15, KJV). The Comforter is here.

Chapter 6

STEPS TO HEALING A BROKEN MARRIAGE

There are many steps to healing a broken marriage. Although you may feel that all is lost or broken, there is no need to fear. God has already ordained a solution in his word for every problem you are facing:

1. Communicating
2. Having Faith
3. Fasting
4. Forbearing each other
5. Loving
6. Praying
7. Pursuing Peace

COMMUNICATING

Lack of communication is cited as the number one reason for divorce (Huff Post Life, 2015). We often like to think it is money or infidelity, but not relating to one another is the biggest problem in a marriage. It is important to set aside quality time to talk to your spouse. Establish family meetings to ensure that each family member's ideas or concerns are heard. It is also important to learn to love your spouse and family. Tell them that you love them and show them your love on a daily basis.

I believe in counseling because the Bible says, "where no counsel is, the people fall: but in the multitude of counsellors there is safety" (Proverbs 11:14, KJV).

The five-fold ministry is ordained by God. "And he gave some, apostles; and some prophets; and some, evangelists; and some, pastors and teachers; For the perfecting of the saints, for the work of the ministry, for the edifying of the body of Christ. Till we all come in the unity of the faith, and of the knowledge of the Son of God into a perfect man, unto the measure of the stature of the fullness of Christ" (Ephesians 4:11-13, KJV).

We are the Body of Christ; we can't say we don't need each other. So, working as a team is God's design in marriage and ministry. "Two are better than one; because they have a good reward for their labour. For if they fall, the one will lift up his fellow: but woe to him that is alone when he falleth; for he hath not another to help him up. Again, if two lie together, then they have heat: but how can one be warm alone? And if one prevail against him, two shall withstand him; and a three-fold cord is not quickly broken" (Ecclesiastes 4:9-12, KJV).

When dealing with conflicts in the family, use a calm voice. We may get angry, but it is very important to calm down first. If you are wrong, say, "I'm sorry. Please forgive me."

Attempt to deal with one problem at a time, rather than lumping all your conflicts into one ball. Try crossing out one problem at a time.

Avoid name-calling, which creates a more hostile environment.

Deal with issues as they arise. Small fires can grow into huge wildfires.

Appreciate each other and what your spouse does at all times. This step is extremely important.

Avoid conflicts by being sensitive to the needs of one another and all others involved. This sensitivity extends to the children in a blended marriage.

It is important to continue to communicate about what to do until you can find the right solution by seeking God. Be patient with each other and ask God for the grace to wait on the solution.

Being honest is an important factor in communicating. When you go to the doctor, you don't say your head hurts when it is your foot that really hurts.

Choose an acceptable time and place for voicing your concerns with your spouse. It's okay to say, "Let's talk about this after the children are in bed." Hopefully, by this point, you both can give your full attention to your relationship and not be distracted.

Turn off the television. Turn off your phones.

If possible, before your discussion, fix a good dinner. Try to find a time when both of you are well rested.

Remember, a soft answer turns away wrath.

Prayer is always the first step. Praying together inserts a calming balm as you are pledging to God to come to a resolution of your differences.

Compromise on the part of the husband and wife may be necessary.

CONFLICT RESOLUTION

Conflict resolution is a way of finding common ground and resolving problems. Following these steps will allow couples to resolve their problems and not destroy each other. The result can be a win-win situation. Using conflict resolution will lead to happier solutions because you are setting out to settle a problem—not to destroy the other person.

1. _Agree on the problem_ – Each should describe the problem as each of them see it. Then, look for a larger issue and any underlying fears and needs. Pick one battle at a time.

2. _Choose environment, rules and boundaries_ – Begin the discussion in a neutral territory such as at a restaurant. Set a time limit for your discussion. Focus on one problem—don't bring in other problems to the discussion. Remain calm and agree to disagree, if needed. Decide on no name calling, belittling of ideas or manipulative behavior.

3. _Gather information_ – Use SWOT (strengths, weaknesses, opportunities, threats). Consider what strengths / weaknesses the other person has that will help in this situation. Is there an opportunity for growth? Who or what might threaten success?

4. _Brainstorm solutions_ – Initially, focus on keeping everything positive. Be creative and stay in the

5. present. Be careful to withhold criticism and instead welcome unusual solutions. Next, focus on turning problems into possibilities, improving on ideas, and combining concepts.

6. _Negotiate_ – Work toward a collaborative solution by being hard on the problem and soft on the person. Then, emphasize the common ground in your argument. Make clear agreements on small things. If necessary, be willing to forgive or ask for forgiveness. This is the time to let go of inconsequential things. Most importantly, allow time for each party to speak and listen.

HAVING FAITH

Faith is a deep belief in things that you cannot see. Faith is what sustains the spirit and provides a link with God. Faith in a higher power is a crucial part of life, and, of course, is vital in a marriage.

A marriage that joins partners in faith will be strong and can weather many difficult problems.

—"So then faith (cometh) by hearing, and hearing by the word of God" (Romans 10:17, KJV). "But without faith [it is] impossible to please Him: for he that cometh to God must believe that He is, and [that] He is a rewarder of them that diligently seek Him" (Hebrews 11:6, KJV).

"That your faith should not stand in the wisdom of men, but in the power of God" (1 Corinthians 2:5, KJV). "For we walk by faith, not by sight" (2 Corinthians 5:7).

Faith is the most important Biblical principle to keep a marriage together. You must have faith at the forefront of everything, especially in your marriage. The Bible says, "Now faith is the substance of things hoped for, the evidence of things not seen" (Hebrews 11:1, KJV).

At times, your spouse will not be the man or woman of your dreams. However, it is important that you begin to visualize and see your spouse as you would like to see him or her in faith. Use your faith to see your spouse as you would hope for your partner to be. You cannot change people, but you can dream, imagine, and meditate on the good contributions and pray for help with the bad.

The gift of God is living waters. You are in a marriage and you are thirsty, and you need fulfillment. No man or woman can totally fulfill the soul, heart, or mind. God is a jealous God. Put God first and then fulfillment comes. Marriage is a legal, binding union between a male and a female. Remember, the blessing of marriage is an assignment and honor from God.

When two are walking in agreement with the purpose of the God: It is:

A mixture

A combination

A connection

A merging

A coupling

A unification

A wedlock

A marriage

An association

An alliance

Marriage is established with rights and obligations between each other. God gives us benefits daily. God has a lot to say about marriage. He is the author of this lifetime institution, and He ordained this marriage contract between a man and a woman. Marriage is also a gift from God not to be taken for granted. It is His gift to us to build a family.

FASTING

Fasting can break the enemy's strongholds in our marriages. When a couple marries, they are certainly not perfect. Moreover, due to past relationships, you may bring in heartache, lack of forgiveness, and hatred. Division is the key problem. Deliverance is necessary as we grow in grace. Fasting has benefits, God pours out His spirit.

"Be not deceived; God is not mocked; for whatsoever a man soweth, that shall he also reap. For he that soweth to his flesh shall of the flesh reap corruption; but he that soweth to the Spirit shall of the Spirit reap life everlasting. And let us not be weary and well doing, for in due season, we shall reap if we faint not" (Galatians 6:7-8, KJV).

"Is not this the fast that I have chosen? To loose the bands of wickedness, to undo heavy burdens, to let the oppressed go free, and that ye break every yoke?" (Isaiah 58:6, KJV). "But thou when thou fasteth, anoint thine head and wash thy face, but unto thy father which is in secret: and thy father, which seeth in secret shall reward you openly" (Matthew 6:17, KJV).

Fasting helps rid us of familial generational curses that have plagued us. Curses get in the way of having a loving, healthy, and nurturing relationship.

There are several Biblical ways to fast, but I would encourage you to fast consulting each other as a couple and watch for the difference it makes in your life. It is important to fast for problems in your marriage such as lust, financial struggles, resentment, jealousy, bitterness, and pride. The flesh always wants its own way. It will never be satisfied.

FORBEARING EACH OTHER

Forbearing is a word that most of us rarely use. It means to refrain, to hold back, to be patient or self-controlled when things annoy or provoke us. The Bible also tells us to constantly forbear one another. "Forbearing one another, and forgiving one another, if any man have a quarrel against any: even as Christ forgave you, so also do ye" (Colossians 3:13, KJV). "With all lowliness and meekness, with longsuffering, forbearing one another in love" (Ephesians 4:2, KJV).

I believe God knew there would be people who would push our buttons and vex our spirits, something those closest to us can be especially good at. Therefore, he tells us that, "A soft answer turneth away wrath: but grievous words stir up anger" (Proverbs 15:1, KJV). We must be meek when someone is upsetting us. This can be a very challenging task for us. However, it is important that we control our anger and get in a habit of being patient with our spouses. No matter how negative the circumstances, we face, we must repent when we need to.

DON'T ALLOW ANGER TO RULE IN YOUR HEART

When we do not release anger in our hearts, we have resentment. Resentment is holding on to past hurts in a relationship, and this causes us to hold grudges. This resentment eventually turns into anger. The end result brings separation and divorce. It is important to not let resentment and anger build up, especially in a marriage.

LOVING

Love is the key to unlocking a successful marriage. We have read the following love chapter at numerous weddings, but applying this chapter (1 Corinthians 13:1-13, KJV) to our marriage is the key to success.

> *"Though I speak with the tongues of men and angels, and have not charity (love) I am become as sounding brass, or a tinkling cymbal. And though I have the gift of prophecy, and understand all mysteries, and all knowledge; and though I have all faith, so that I could remove mountains, and have not charity (love), I am nothing.*
>
> *"And though I bestow all my goods to feed the poor, and though I give my body to be burned, and have not charity (love), it profiteth me nothing.*
>
> *"Charity (love) suffereth long and is kind; charity (love) envieth not; charity (love) vaunteth not itself, it is not puffed up.*
>
> *"Doth not behave itself unseemly, seeketh not her own, is not easily provoked, thinketh no evil;*
>
> *"Rejoiceth not in iniquity, but rejoiceth in truth;*
>
> *"Beareth all things, believeth all things. Hopeth all things, endureth all things.*

"Charity never faileth: but whether there be prophecies, they shall fail; whether there be tongues, they shall cease; whether there be knowledge, it shall vanish away.

"For we know in part, and we prophecy in part.

"But when that which is perfect is come, then that which is in part shall be done away.

"When I was a child, I spake as a child. I understood as a child, I thought as a child: but when I became a man, I put away childish things.

"For now we see through a glass, darkly; but then face to face: now I know in part; but then shall I know even as also I am known.

"And now abideth faith, hope, charity, these three; but the greatest of these is charity."

A number of us are in loveless marriages. Sometimes this is our fault. We cut ourselves off from our spouses emotionally, sexually, and financially. Before we recognize what has happened to us, we are no longer in love with our spouse. More importantly, it is difficult to find our way back to a loving relationship. When this break up occurs, it is critical to pray and find your way back by prayer and fasting and communicating with your spouse and "believing" in hope, before it is too late.

PRAYING

Don't forget to pray daily. If our marriage is to be successful, we must learn to pray together as a family. We should pray before we start each day and at the end of our day. Pray from your heart unto God. "Confess your faults one to another, and pray one for another, that ye may be healed. The effectual fervent prayer of a righteous man availeth much" (James 5:16, KJV).

A good prayer life will help you on your journey to success. The prayers do not have to be long. Remember, we are on assignment and our task is to fulfill our role as married partners to be what God intended us to be in the earthly realm. By praying as a family unit, we are showing our gratitude to God and gratitude for our family. We are thanking God for our health, safety, finances and wealth. By praying, we are requesting forgiveness from God, forgiveness from each other, and deliverance for ourselves from temptation and evil. We are also praising God the Father, in Jesus' name, for our blessings.

PURSUING PEACE

The path of peace is what we want to pursue. Jesus came so that men might have peace on earth. Even though there is confusion in many places, pursuing peace and allowing the peace of God to rule in our hearts and minds is essential.

Life's demands can be overwhelming. The Bible offers many verses on peace, such as Job 22:21-22, KJV, "Acquaint now thyself with Him, and be at peace: thereby good shall come unto thee." Receive instructions from His mouth, and lay up His words in your heart. Living according to the word of God by faith gives us peace.

Chapter 7

HOW TO SEEK GOD IN YOUR MARRIAGE TO DEAL WITH PROBLEMS

WHO ARE YOU TO GOD?

God is our creator—Man is His creation.
God is infinite. Man is finite.
God is self-sufficient. Man is totally dependent on God.
God never errs. Man often errs.

(Romans 9:19-23, KJV)

As we seek God in our marriage, do not be surprised when we face personality traits in our spouse that are not favorable. All marriages have challenges and conflicts. These challenges often come in various areas. It is important for us to be aware of the traits and behaviors that can cause grief in our marriage. We can overcome these problems by using Biblical principles or remedies.

The devil is trying to destroy marriages. However, I am here in the name of Jesus, to destroy the Kingdom of Darkness. To effectively deal with the Kingdom of Hell's antics and devices, we must; "Dress accordingly in the spirit" and "Be obedient to the word of God which is God," as written in Ephesians 6:11-20, KJV.

11. "Put on the whole armour of God so that ye may be able to stand against the wiles of the devil." Wiles means a trick or strategy meant to fool or trap you through beguiling behavior or trickery.
12. "For we wrestle not against flesh and blood, but against principalities, against powers, against the rulers of the darkness of this world, against spiritual wickedness in high places"
13. "Wherefore take unto you the whole armour of God, that ye may be able to withstand in the evil day, and having done all, stand"
14. "Stand therefore, having your loins girt about with truth, and having on the breastplate of righteousness"
15. "And your feet shod with the preparation of the gospel of peace"
16. "Above all, taking the shield of faith, wherewith ye shall be able to quench all the fiery darts of the wicked"
17. "And take the helmet of salvation, and the sword of the Spirit, which is the word of God"
18. "Praying always with all prayer and supplication in the Spirit, and watching thereunto with all perseverance and supplication for all saints"
19. "And for me, that utterance may be given unto me, that I may open my mouth boldly, to make known the mystery of the gospel"
20. "For which I am an ambassador in bonds: that therein I may speak boldly as I ought to speak"

Spiritual warfare is real. As believers in Jesus Christ, the Messiah, we fail to note that we are fighting an army who we cannot see. We deal with this on a daily basis, and we must use the sword of the spirit, which is the word of God. The assignment of any enemy is to destroy.

If we are not prepared by putting on the helmet of salvation, we will not be able to stand. The helmet of salvation is our hope in Jesus Christ. We must be eternally hopeful despite our circumstances. It is important for us to put on the helmet of righteousness. We are called to be righteous. "But be ye doers of the word, and not bearers only, deceiving your own selves" (James 1:22, KJV).

I have touched on a few of these scenarios. However, there are many more devils that you may need to fight and wrestle with. The key is to fight using all of the principles outlined above.

DEALING WITH A "MOMMA'S BOY"

Most women have trouble with "momma's boys." These men have difficulties establishing boundaries with their mothers or caregivers. This can present major challenges in the communication between a man and his wife. Generally, a "momma's boy" does not make a move without the permission of his mother. This can create huge communication obstacles in a marriage. Therefore, it is important to get these issues on the table when they present themselves. Pastoral counseling is helpful (especially for new couples) to deal with the difficulties of these types of relationships. Again, it is important to pray through these problems.

DEALING WITH A JEZEBEL SPIRIT

Some women domineer over their spouse. We call this the *Jezebel spirit*. Jezebel was married to King Ahab, and instead of Ahab getting his direction and instructions from God, Ahab listened to his wife. As a result, Israel turned its back on God. This nation, which was recognized to be a nation of God-fearing people, began to suffer under Ahab's leadership.

Some women may make more money than their spouse, but it does not give them the right to be bossy, domineering, rude, or critical. You should never weaken your partner with words. A woman's duty is to respect her husband, and to build him up. She should pray for an increase in his life both spiritually and naturally.

"The wicked, through the pride of his countenance, will not seek after God: God is not in all his thoughts" (Psalms 10:4, KJV). There is no need to be prideful and unloving. God dislikes pride, and we all know it goeth before a fall. We must be humble to God and submit to one another, in the fear of God. "The fear of the Lord is to hate evil: pride, and arrogancy, and the evil way, and the forward mouth, do I hate" (Proverbs 8:13, KJV). "Only by pride cometh contention: but with the well advised is wisdom" (Proverbs 13:10, KJV). "The fear of the Lord is the instruction of wisdom; and before honour is humility" (Proverbs 15:33, KJV).

Men, when you are faced with this type of woman, you are to pray and to cast that spirit out. An arrogant and unsubmitted woman is definitely not part of God's design for a marriage.

HANDLING ISSUES OF SUBSTANCE ABUSE AND MENTAL HEALTH IN A MARRIAGE

In today's society, drugs and alcohol are prevalent. Additionally, there is a greater stress on families to manage their household. A consequence of these two concerns is a greater reliance on drugs and alcohol. This manifests itself in behaviors that are most harmful to the family unit. A lot of marriages suffer when one spouse is battling addiction.

A number of people turn to drugs because they are suffering from mental health issues such as depression, anxiety, and other mental health concerns. Some of these problems are serious and will require a husband or wife to search for the right answers with mental health practitioners. Despite these circumstances, the word of God has the ultimate answers. We need to search the scriptures daily and seek the Holy Spirit for the best solution. Put on your garment of Praise " ...for the spirit of heaviness" (Isaiah 61:3, KJV). Dealing with depression is real. Even in the depths of despair, remember, we have someone to rejoice in, the Lord, we stand in the faith of Jesus Christ. The Word states in Philippians 4:4-13, KJV:

> 4. *"Rejoice in the Lord always; and again, I say, Rejoice"*
> (Philippians 4:13, KJV).

> 5. *"Let your moderation be known unto all men. The Lord is at hand"*
> (Philippians 4:14, KJV).

> 6. *"Be careful for nothing; but in every thing by prayer and supplication with thanksgiving let your requests be made known unto God"*
> (Philippians 4:15, KJV).

> 7. *"And the peace of God, which passeth all understanding, shall keep your hearts and minds through Christ Jesus"*
> (Philippians 4:16, KJV).

> 8. *"Finally, brethren, whatsoever things are true, whatsoever things are honest, whatsoever things are just, whatsoever things are pure, whatsoever things are lovely,*

whatsoever things are of good report, if there be any virtue, and if there be any praise think on these things"
(Philippians 4:17, KJV).

9. *"Those things which you have both learned, and received, and heard, and seen in me, do: and the God of peace shall be with you"*
(Philippians 4:18, KJV).

10. *"But I rejoiced in the Lord greatly, that now at the last your care of me hath flourished again; wherein you were also careful, but ye lacked opportunity"*
(Philippians 4:19, KJV).

11. *"Not that I speak in respect of want: for I have learned, in whatsoever state I am, therewith to be content"*
(Philippians 4:20, KJV).

12. *"I know both how to be abased, and I know how to abound: everywhere and in all things I am instructed both to be full and to be hungry, both to abound and to suffer need"*
(Philippians 4:21, KJV).

13. *"I can do all things through Christ which strengtheneth me"*
(Philippians 4:22, KJV).

LUST AND PORNOGRAPHY IN A MARRIAGE RELATIONSHIP

We must put some passions and desires to death. The flesh is sinful and weak. We must examine our flesh in our marriages. "Now the works of the flesh are manifest, which are these; Adultery, fornication, uncleanness, lasciviousness, idolatry, witchcraft, hatred, variance, emulations, wrath, strife, seditions, heresies, envying, murderers, drunkenness, revellings, and such like: of the which I tell you before, as I have also told you in times past, that they which do such things shall not inherit the kingdom of God" (Galatians 5:19-21, KJV).

It is important not to allow lust in your marriage. Lust is the flesh having a very strong sexual desire. You have a sexual drive to engage in sexual relationships with a woman who is not your wife. You crave, you covet; you want to be with her and forsake your covenant because of your hunger to be with someone other than your spouse.

We must remember that watching pornography is an open door to destroying your marriage. Women, watching man-to-man coupling, lusting after someone either on the job or the grocery store or your husband's hot male friend can lead you down a path that will destroy your marriage. Women and men, you should not discuss your sex lives with your friends. This can be a disaster.

HANDLING CHILDREN IN A MARRIAGE

The Bible says, "Train up a child in the way he should go: and when he is old, he will not depart from it" (Proverbs 22:6, KJV). There is a divine order for the Godly family. Being a real husband requires that you will seek the heart of God for your family. That husband will start the process by loving his wife and children.

It is important that children remember the role of the father at all times, and this is not only important for the children, but also for the wife. Remember, the father is the head of the family. The role of the father is given to him by God. Unfortunately, men and some women tend to put the children ahead of the husband and ahead of the spouse.

This is not the proper alignment in God's kingdom. Do not allow division in your home. Children should be taught to show respect to the husband and wife of the household.

Many are in blended families, and you must accept all the children. Do not allow division because a spouse does not accept a child from a previous marriage or relationship. It could be a child that is your own, but because one spouse loves the child so much it causes dissension.

Because of what to reveal and what not to reveal to the children about the marriage, you and your spouse should set ground rules when parenting children. For example, once a decision is made concerning the child, you and your spouse should stick with that decision.

Lastly, teach your children:

1. "Children obey your parents in the Lord: for this is right.
2. "Honour thy father and mother (which is the first commandment with promise)
3. "That it may be well with thee, and thou mayest live long on the earth" (Ephesians 6:1-3, KJV).

Fathers, "provoke not your children to wrath: but bring them up in the nurture and admonition of the Lord" (Ephesians 6:4, KJV). These Biblical principles will serve the child and the parent in the long run. This last verse is often forgotten by a parent who may be overbearing. We must be careful to always discipline our children with love.

HANDLING A SPOUSE WHO WANTS A SEPARATION OR DIVORCE

At times in a marriage, the words separation or divorce come up. This is a tough time, especially when one or neither party wants to divorce. Remember to pray, fast, communicate, love, have faith, forbear, and do not allow anger to reign in your heart. If all else fails, then I would recommend that you accept it. I recommend that you follow the principles above when these two words are mentioned. Allowing the Holy Spirit to lead and guide you is the first priority.

Make certain that others are not in your spouse's ear, such as your mother, father, brother, sister, other extended family members, friends, or foes.

Discussing the dissolution of a marriage is a painful experience. It is important that both spouses have tried to do everything in their power to save the marriage. Divorce was never God's will. However, because of the hardening of the hearts, marriages are sometimes dissolved.

Ray Stedman, author of *Authentic Christianity*, stated, "Grounds for divorce include adultery and unbelief."

> *"And unto the married I command, yet not I, but the Lord,*
> *Let not the wife depart from her husband"*
> (1 Corinthians 7:10, KJV).

It says in Leviticus 18:6-18, KJV,

6. "None of you shall approach to any that is near of kin to him, to uncover their nakedness: I am the Lord."
7. "The nakedness of thy father or the nakedness of thy mother, shalt thou not uncover: she is thy mother; shalt thou not uncover: she is thy mother; thou shalt not uncover her nakedness."
8. "The nakedness of thy father's wife shalt thou not uncover: it is thy father's nakedness."
9. "The nakedness of thy sister, the daughter of thy father, or daughter of thy mother, whether she be born at home, or born abroad, even their nakedness thou shalt not uncover."

10. "The nakedness of thy son's daughter, or of thy daughter's daughter, even their nakedness thou shalt not uncover: for theirs is thine own nakedness."

11. "The nakedness of thy father's wife's daughter, begotten by thy father, she is thy sister, thou shalt not uncover her nakedness."

12. "Thou shalt not uncover the nakedness of thy father's sister: she is thy father's near kinswoman."

13. "Thou shalt not uncover the nakedness of thy mother's sister: for she is thy mother's near kinswoman."

14. "Thou shalt not uncover the nakedness of thy father's brother, thou shalt not approach to his wife: she is thine aunt."

15. "Thou shalt not uncover the nakedness of thy daughter in law: she is thy son's wife; thou shalt not uncover her nakedness."

16. "Thou shalt not uncover the nakedness of thy brother's wife: it is thy brother's nakedness."

17. "Thou shalt not uncover the nakedness of a woman and her daughter, neither shalt thou take her son's daughter, or her daughter's daughter, to uncover her nakedness; for they are her near kinswomen: it is wickedness."

18. "Neither shalt thy take a wife to her sister, to vex her, to uncover her nakedness, beside the other in her life time."

Deuteronomy says,

"For the Lord thy God walketh in the midst of thy camp, to deliver thee, and to give up thine enemies before thee; therefore shall the camp be holy: that he see no unclean thing in thee, and turn away from thee" (Deuteronomy 23:14, KJV).

DEALING WITH ILLNESS AND DEATH

Unfortunately, there will come a time when one must deal with sickness such as a debilitating disease or, unfortunately, the death of a spouse. Of course, this is a difficult time for the spouse, who, for example, is left handling the illness of his or her spouse. Prayer and faith are required, and submitting to the will of God at all times is very important. I have personally dealt with the illness and death of my husband, and though it is difficult, you can recover.

The Bible says, "Is any among you afflicted? Let him call for the elders of the church; and let them pray over him, anointing him with oil in the name of the Lord" (James 5:14, KJV).

Chapter 8

FINDING WAYS TO KEEP YOUR MARRIAGE EXCITING

How do you keep your marriage exciting? It is important to always date your spouse. They are your true love. And, it's always important to keep the love flowing.

WHAT DO MEN WANT?

Men are complex. Some have simple desires, and if you ask them what they want out of a wife, they will give you very simple answers. Others are very complicated, and understanding them requires patience and lots of love and prayer. So, the wife should communicate with her husband. The following are the things most men want from their wives:

1. A woman who cooks, or knows what to prepare for his meals
2. A woman who cleans, or makes sure the job is done
3. A woman who pleases him without withholding herself sexually
4. A woman who takes great care of her children and trains them

5. A woman who plans ahead and meets necessary obligations
6. A woman who prays for and with him, who his heart can trust

WHAT DO WOMEN WANT?

1. A man who says something special to her when she gets up in the morning. His words should be kind words.
2. A man who treats her as if she is the most important person on the planet
3. A man who pays attention to her and listens to her cries
4. A man who listens to her heart and hears what she is speaking or concerned about, and helps her find a solution
5. A man who treats her to romantic dinners, exercise, trips, movies, or whatever she likes, that is edifying for positive growth in the family unit

Basically, each should know or be creative in how to amuse each other.

HOW TO HAVE A PROSPEROUS MARRIAGE

God gave us a condition for a blessing. God will bless all the works of our hands in all that we do (Deuteronomy 28, KJV). We can have success in our lives if we diligently hearken to the voice and obey His commandments. The Lord, your God, gives you the power to get wealth. You have authority over your emotions, power over the spirit of lust, and most importantly, power over your mind. Focus your mind on Jesus and the Lord will establish you, strengthen you, and settle you for His glory. "But you will receive power, after that the Holy Ghost is come upon you" (Acts 1:8, KJV).

Every marriage has the potential to survive if God is put first. Every man and woman has the potential for a successful marriage, if each partner believes. The hidden seeds of potential are in everyone, if you don't hinder the process. God wants to give us a life of abundance. "I am come that they might have life, and that they might have it more abundantly" (John 10:10, KJV).

It is important to remember to accept change in a marriage, and in life, at times. Change is necessary. Ruth and Naomi, due to the death of their husbands, had to move. Ruth moved away from Moab with her mother in-law because her father-in-law, husband, and brother-in-law had all died. Naomi served God, and she suggested that Ruth find another husband. Ruth followed Naomi and said that, " ...where thou goest, I will go, and where though lodgest, I will lodge: thy people shall be my people, and thy God, my God. " (Ruth 1:16, KJV). Ruth stayed true to Naomi, and as a result, she met Boaz in Bethlehem.

Look at God, our Creator. He called the dry land earth, and the gathering of the waters he called the seas. God gave Adam dominion over our environment (Genesis 1:26-28, KJV). We have chaos in the world because of the war between God and Lucifer. When Lucifer rebelled, he took the angels, and they were cast out of heaven (Revelation 12:9, KJV). Through the blood of Jesus Christ, we can have the victory in marriage, and can overcome any obstacles. Use the dominion that God gave you through Jesus Christ to overcome any obstacles that you or your family encounter.

TAKE COURAGE

Take courage, my friend, it will not be long.
You will be able to sing a brand new song.
The joy of Jesus is the life we live.
Peace and safety that's what he gives.

Comforter on every side,

His eternal word is our guide.

He will strengthen you and bless you too.

Faithful and true is our King who opens doors.

Yes, he knows everything.

God sees and knows what you do not know.

He goes where you cannot go.

God is a spirit who can see

Everything about you and me.

If you have faith and can believe,

That is all He asks of thee.

So, trust His word, live right, be strong,

Pray each day as you go along.

BE BLESSED

The Hebrew word for blessed is barak, pronounced baw-rahk. I pronounce a blessing of love and success in your marriage. Blessings have to do with approval. Ask God for protection and favor in your marriage.

One way to bless others is to pray for them to have good things in their lives.

God created life. Life is good because we breathe, we speak, we sing, we dance, and we play. Marriages create a family, which allows us to be able to come together to enjoy each other. We must be thankful each day and be grateful for the life that God has given us, even though we will experience bad things.

BIBLE SCRIPTURES TO RECITE DAILY

It is clear that as a husband, you should love your wife, as Christ loved the church. Jesus Christ gave his life for his bride to become one spirit. "Husbands, love your wives, and be not bitter against them" (Colossians 3:19, KJV). Bitter means things that are hard to bear. These things may be grievous, distressful, or cause pain. When something is bitter, it causes strong antagonism or hostility. People who are bitter feel resentful. Some bitter individuals may be cynical. In terms of food or taste, things that are bitter cause people tasting them to shudder or will not want to eat much of them. Similarly, people who are bitter cause others to shun them. Being around bitter people is not pleasant.

Cain became bitter because of Abel's sacrifice to God was more acceptable. This caused Cain to murder his brother, Abel (Genesis 4:4-5, KJV), The Lord has respect unto Abel and his offering, but unto Cain, and his offering he had not respect and Cain was very wroth, and his countenance fell (Genesis 4:4-5, KJV).

- "Husbands, love your wives, even as Christ also loved the church, and gave himself for it" (Ephesians 5:25, KJV).
- "Likewise, ye husbands, dwell with them according to knowledge, giving honour unto the wife, as unto the weaker vessel, and as being heirs together of the grace of life; that your prayers be not hindered" (1 Peter 3:7, KJV).
- "Wives, submit yourselves unto your own husbands, as unto the Lord. For the husband is the head of the wife, even as Christ is the head of the church: and he is the savior of the body" (Ephesians 5:22-23, KJV).
- "But if any provide not for his own, and specially for those of his own house, he hath denied the faith, and is worse than an infidel" (1 Timothy 5:8, KJV).

- "Live joyfully with the wife whom thou lovest all the days of the life of thy vanity, which he hath given thee under the sun, all the days of thy vanity; for that is thy portion in this life, and in thy labour which thou takest under the sun" (Ecclesiastes 9:9, KJV).
- "For this cause shall a man leave his father and mother, and shall be joined unto his wife, and they two shall be one flesh" (Ephesians 5:31, KJV).

If you are being, abused, accused, battered, broken, beaten, cursed, downtrodden, frightened, forgotten, hindered, or not loved, I suggest you get professional assistance. You can seek professional help from a pastor, a counselor, or a health practitioner. I do not believe that God intended for us to be in or stay in abusive situations or relationships. This includes abuse by men and women.

Men can also be abused, although it happens in smaller numbers than the abuse of women.

God calls us to love and to care for our spouses as Christ loved the church. If we are abusing someone, whether verbal or physical abuse, that is not an indication of love. As the Bible says in scripture: "Love is patient, love is kind" (1 Corinthians 13:4, KJV). If anything, other than what the scripture says is occurring in your relationship, then seek help.

YOU CAN MAKE IT

If you cannot see, you should not drive,
If you cannot love her, she should not ride.
So, put away your foolish pride
and let the Holy Spirit be your guide.
You can make it, whatever comes your way.
That's the will of God for you, each and every day.

Seek Him and you shall find, I speak joy
and peace to your mind.
Will God be late? Does God not see?
God knows everything about you and me.
So, we bow down, now to pray,
And learn to praise the Lord every day.

BIBLIOGRAPHY

Dictionary.com

Gladden, Alfred P. *Taste Bud—Tidbits: What You Eat—or What's Eating You? One Man's Revelations.* 2008. Self-Published.

King James Bible.

Poor Communication is the #1 Reason Couples Split up: Survey. Huff Post Life, November 20, 2013. https://www.huffpost.com/entry/divorcecauses-_n_4304466

Steadman, Ray C. *Authentic Christianity.* 2008. Harrisburg, Pennsylvania: Discovery House.

APPENDIX: INSIGHTS ON WHAT GOD REQUIRES OF US

CREATION OF MALE AND FEMALE

The birth of man was on the sixth day of creation, after all the living creatures were made. "So God created man in his own image, in the image of God created him, male and female created them he" (Genesis 1:27, KJV).

"In the beginning was the word, and the word was with God, and the word was God" (John 1:1, KJV). "And the Lord God formed man of the dust of the ground, and breathed into his nostrils, the breath of life; and man became a living soul" (Genesis 2:7, KJV).

Adam was alone, giving names to all the animals, fowls of the air, cattle, and all other beasts God had made out of the ground. But Adam did not have a helpmate. "And the Lord God said, It is not good that the man should be alone; I will make him an help meet for him" (Genesis 2:18, KJV). "And the Lord God caused a deep sleep to fall upon Adam, and he slept: and He took one of his ribs, and closed up the flesh instead thereof; And the rib, which the Lord God had taken from man, made he a woman, and brought her unto the man" (Genesis 2:21-22, KJV). Even today, God knows how to bring the wife unto the man.

Most cultures recognize marriage and the partners in marriage—husband and wife.

THE ASSIGNMENT OF MAN

We are body, soul, and spirit. God declared His purpose for man and our assignment at hand. The assignment is clear, God spoke by His spirit and created life as He breathed into Adam's nostrils. "And God blessed them, and God said unto them, Be fruitful, and multiply, and replenish the earth, and subdue it: and have dominion over the fish of the sea, and over the fowl of the air, and over every living thing that moveth upon the earth" (Genesis 1:28, KJV).

Our Creator has multi-faceted attributes. "And God said unto Moses, I am that I am: and he said, Thus shalt thou say unto the children of Israel, I am hath sent me unto you" (Exodus 3:14, KJV). "God is a spirit, and they that worship him must worship him in spirit and in truth" (John 4:24, KJV). God's illustration is a clear picture of Himself, for us to develop faith in a creator we cannot see.

GOD IS OUR SUBSTANCE

It is possible, as we seek Him with all our hearts, to allow Him to reveal His existence and our purpose on earth. "He is our substance!" Apostle Sharlene Jones preached this at the Remnant Church, for the body of Christ. "Now faith is the substance of things hoped for, the evidence of things not seen" (Hebrews 11:1, KJV). A Psalm of David to the chief musician made it clear in Psalms 19:1, KJV, "The heavens declare the glory of God; and the firmament sheweth his handiwork." So, when the devil asks you where is your God? He is in the heavens judging right. We will eternally one day get there, because heaven knows how to get us there. That is our faith.

YOU MUST BE BORN AGAIN

Enter in, receive the word of God. You must be born again to be partakers of the kingdom of God. Nicodemus, a ruler of the Jews, a man of the Pharisees, asked Jesus a question because of His miracles. "Jesus answered and said unto him, Verily, verily, I say unto thee, Except a man be born again, he cannot see the kingdom of God" (John 3:3, KJV). So, I pray that God will open up the eyes of your understanding, as you seek him with all your heart. He is near. Make the call, seek the Lord, while you have breath in your lungs. He will not cast you away. His arms are stretched out for you! God's word has been tested. "Jesus saith unto him, I am the way, the truth, and the life: no man cometh unto the Father, but by me" (John 14:6, KJV).

THE WAR AND THE ENEMY

The god of the kingdom of darkness has clouded the minds of those who do not believe in the gospel of Jesus Christ. "But if our gospel be hid, it is hid to them that are lost: In whom the God of this world hath blinded the minds of them which believe not, lest the light of the glorious gospel of Christ, who is the image of God, should shine upon them" (2 Corinthians 4:3-4, KJV).

Satan has fought the plan of God and man against the Creator from the beginning of time. "And there was war in heaven: Michael and his angels fought against the dragon; and the dragon fought and his angels, and prevailed not; neither was their place found any more in heaven. And the great dragon was cast out, that old serpent, called the Devil, and Satan, which deceiveth the whole world: he was cast out into the earth, and his angels were cast out with him" (Revelation 12:7-9, KJV). "And he said unto them, I beheld Satan as lightning fall from heaven.

Behold, I give unto you power to tread on serpents and scorpions, and over all the power of the enemy: and nothing shall by any means hurt you" (Luke 10:18-19, KJV).

What was the devil's downfall? "Pride goeth before destruction, and an haughty spirit before a fall" (Proverbs 16:18-19, KJV). Satan is a defeated enemy before God. He will never overthrow God or His people. He is the opposite of all that God is, he is backward, perverse; he is the door to hell and destruction. That will never change. He is going to the bottomless pit. The angels will see to it. "And he opened the bottomless pit; and there arose a smoke out of the pit, as the smoke of a great furnace; and the sun and the air were darkened by reason of the smoke of the pit" (Revelation 9:2 KJV).

Satan's kingdom can hold us in captivity, keep us blind to the truth of his existence, and keep confusion in the minds of men. Enter into the kingdom of light, it expels the darkness on earth that wants to hold you captive in word and by thought and deeds. Satan is the thief and his plan is destruction. "The thief cometh not, but for to steal, and to kill, and to destroy: I am come that they might have life, and that they might have it more abundantly" (John 10:10, KJV).

Adam and Eve disobeyed God in the garden of Eden, so we were all born in sin and shaped in iniquity. Satan will keep you drunk, wavering, doubtful, fearful, and without faith. So, be sober and be alert. Believe the gospel of Jesus Christ. "Be not deceived; God is not mocked: for whatsoever a man soweth, that shall he also reap" (Galatians 6:7, KJV). Let the cruel mockers keep on mocking, as they willfully cause pain and discomfort to others.

God will protect and strengthen you, and deal with the enemies of the cross. The devil wants to discourage you—to defeat your purpose and your faith in the word of God. Walk in the path of righteousness. Why am I saying all this? I don't want you to be unlearned, unaware, or blind to the words of darkness. The devil will try to destroy a merging, a union of two becoming one; anything that will expose his kingdom. Satan will especially work against marriage. However, the power of two in agreement is a mighty force against evil. That is a big threat to the enemy.

The battle, the war is not against flesh and blood. "For we wrestle not against flesh and blood, but against principalities, against powers, against the rulers of the darkness of this world, against spiritual wickedness in high places" (Ephesians 6:12, KJV). All false gods must fall! All lies must fall! "Let God arise, let his enemies be scattered: let them also that hate him flee before him. As smoke is driven away, so drive them away: as wax melted before the fire, so let the wicked perish at the presence of God" (Psalm 68:1-2, KJV).

"He that committeth sin is of the devil; for the devil sinneth from the beginning. For this purpose the Son of God was manifested, that he might destroy the works of the devil" (1 John 3:8, KJV). Submit to the word of God! If you follow evil, Satan is your father. He is the father of lies. "Ye are of your father the devil, and the lusts of your father ye will do. He was a murderer from the beginning, and abode not in the truth, because there is no truth in him. When he speaketh a lie, he speaketh of his own: for he is a liar, and the father of it" (John 8:44, KJV).

JESUS CHRIST'S LOVE FOR MANKIND

The death of Jesus Christ abolished the penalty for all our sins. By the shedding of the blood of Jesus Christ, the debt is paid in full. Jesus made the exchange while we were yet sinners. Jesus Christ died for our sins. Faith in the Lord Jesus Christ, who was crucified, rescued us from every scheme, lie, plot, or deception. We are vindicated! Just repent daily and trust the Bible. "Know ye not, that to whom ye yield yourselves servants to obey; whether of sin unto death, or of obedience unto righteousness?"

(Romans 6:16, KJV). "Submit yourselves therefore to God. Resist the devil, and he will flee from you" (James 4:7, KJV).

Agree with God! Love God with all you've got! Put God first. He will not fail you! I have been saved for forty years, since March, 1980. I have found no failure in God! God is faithful to all who trust Him. God hears and answers. If you have fallen, get up! "For a just man falleth seven times, and riseth up again: but the wicked shall fall into mischief" (Proverbs 24:16, KJV).

ABOUT THE AUTHOR

A picture of the Author.

Carla was born in Clovis, New Mexico as Carla Liverman. Her dad was a career military man. Carla called her mother, his beautiful wife, "Queen." The family lived in Great Falls, Montana, and then moved to Baltimore, Maryland, after the loss of her four-year-old brother when Carla was eight-years of age. After this tragedy and her father retiring from military service, her parents divorced though they later remarried.

Carla had another brother who was shot, and his last words to her were, "Carla, stay in the church. I know you are saved because you could never dance." She also had two other sisters. However, her life was not easy.

At age twelve, Carla was kicked out of the choir and told she was "out of tune." When she was fourteen, she gave birth to her own miracle. Her son, Robert, was her blessing. He grew up to be a responsible man and now has three sons of his own: the twins, Reggie and Robert, and their brother, Cortland.

When Carla was twenty-five and had accepted Jesus Christ as her savior, Carla was kicked out of her house. Later, her father got saved. Years later, Carla performed his celebration of life and made a good prayer warrior out of him with the love of Pastor Dorothy Banks, along with Candy Brown who prayed with her three times a day.

Carla graduated from Edmondson High School in Baltimore, Maryland, and attended many colleges as she traveled to better herself. She has visited every state in the United States except California, the place she was headed to further her modeling career. She was saved when she was working in a bar.

She became an usher at the Tabernacle of Prayer Church for three years, where she later married Evangelist Tony Wilson. Pastor/Evangelist Tony Wilson and Evangelist Carla Wilson founded the Church of Jesus Christ in the Power of God Ministry located in Baltimore. The first five years Carla studied the Bible as her job. After that, they spent fifteen years traveling and winning souls for Jesus Christ. They also took in seventeen homeless families, teaching and preaching the gospel with them.

Evangelist Carla Wilson preached a radio ministry at WJRQ 1590 in Glen Burnie, Maryland, for many years. Carla founded the New Life Family Daycare. She took spiritual warfare training at the Baltimore Bible College. She helped establish the church as she traveled with her husband and Apostle Kerry Jones, Pastor of Jesus Christ Prayer of Deliverance Ministry. She went to Africa on an international mission after training the grandchildren for eight years. She worked with God's Word Will and Way under the Leadership of Pastor Joyce Jones and Tyrone Jones along with Minister Betty Keene.

Pastor Carla Wilson then went into the healthcare field. She led many to Jesus Christ before they departed this life. She worked three years at Simmons Memorial Baptist Church with Pastor Dwayne Simmons, and many became filled with the Holy Spirit while Carla performed street ministry after the passing of her husband, Tony.

She has experienced a variety of adventures and life-threatening situations. She has been choked, had a gun poked in her side, and received many losses. She was called crazy and lost her family and friends and faced many foes. But God, who is rich in mercy, was the steadfast keeper of her soul.

Carla also worked as a patient care technician at Sibley Memorial Hospital in Washington, D.C., and took a buyout so as to continue her ministry. Pastor Carla moved to Broken Arrow, Oklahoma, for five years. As an Evangelist, she served under Dr. Delroy Markand and Pastor Willie Jean Markland. She married a military man, spent ten years trying to save the marriage, rebuilding it four times, until her husband finally said, "you're released."

She now writes poems, songs, and books, praying ever to be humble and holy.

Pastor Banks reminded me **"we must always have Faith and Focus to endure!"**

Our church takes marriage serious! As the senior Pastor at God's Word, Will and Way Ministries, I read this book. God has a word for you. Read this book and you will be blessed!

- Pastor Joyce Jones

Hindering Husbands and Helpless Wives is now available on Amazon.

Audiobook -   A recording of the book!
                   "Your talking book"

e-book -   An electronic book that you can read on your desktop computers, laptops, tablets and smartphones.

Kindle -   Read on your handheld electronic devices.

Hindering Husbands and Helpless Wives will be coming in **Spanish**.

Printed in the United States
by Baker & Taylor Publisher Services